Thomas Hutchinson

Ballades and other Rhymes of a Country Bookworm

Thomas Hutchinson

Ballades and other Rhymes of a Country Bookworm

ISBN/EAN: 9783744775977

Printed in Europe, USA, Canada, Australia, Japan

Cover: Foto ©Thomas Meinert / pixelio.de

More available books at **www.hansebooks.com**

Sixty Copies of this Large Paper Edition have been printed, fifty of which are for sale.

This Copy is No.

Signed,

BALLADES OF A COUNTRY BOOKWORM.

Ballades

AND OTHER RHYMES

OF

A Country Bookworm

BY

THOMAS HUTCHINSON

In the work-a-day world,—for its needs and woes,
There is place and enough for the pains of prose;
But whenever the May-bells clash and chime,
Then hey! for the ripple of laughing rhyme!
—AUSTIN DOBSON.

LONDON:
STANESBY & CO., 173, SLOANE STREET, S.W.
(FORMERLY MURRAY & STANESBY).

DERBY AND NOTTINGHAM
FRANK MURRAY.

1888.

TO ANDREW LANG.

Dear Andrew, with the brindled hair,
* * * * **
I count you happy starred, for God,
When He with ink-pot and with rod
Endowed you, bade your fortune lead
Forever by the crooks of Tweed,
Forever by the woods of song
And lands that to the Muse belong.
—R. L. STEVENSON.

As one who often finds delight
  In Books and Bookmen's bookly lore,
This volume to you I indite
  In hopes it may—at least—not bore:
  To authors who are now no more
You late address'd yourself, but I
  To one alive do much prefer
To speak—to one who ne'er will die.

What I would fain express, perchance,
  I ought not to attempt in rhyme,
Yet do not wish me, say, in France—
  Or in some other warmer clime:
  Not tho' it be in me a crime
A worthless work to you to send—
  You, in your books, time after time,
Have seem'd indeed to me a friend.

TO ANDREW LANG.

I struggle up Parnassus—yes,
  I struggle, that is the right phrase,
For 'tis not easy, I confess,
  To one of my prosaic ways
  To imitate your courtly lays—
To offer in your own sweet style
  My heartfelt wishes: many days
I've thought of it—nay, do not smile.

Long may The Ship by you be steer'd,
  And may you long man's soul enthrall
With tales of bogies that you fear'd
  In childhood—even yet recall
  With trembling lips: oft may you fall
Into temptation, buying books
  At auction-mart, at shop, at stall:
Oft angle in NORTHUMBRIAN brooks.

But, above all, long may you write
  Sketch, ballade, novel, sonnet, song,
Dispelling by each Fancy's flight
  The recollections that belong
  To those whose fellows do them wrong;
And proving that it still is good
  To live, for that Faith makes us strong—
Faith in the Human Brotherhood.

Pegswood, Morpeth.   THOMAS HUTCHINSON.

CONTENTS:

BALLADES.   PAGE.

    Austin Dobson—Andrew Lang 3
    A Christmas Ballade 5
    Ballade of Unrecognized Genius... 7
    A Town-Lover's Ballade 9
    Ballade of a Poor Book-Lover 11
    Ballade of a Muffin-Seller 13
    Ballade addressed to George Augustus Sala ... 15
    Ballade of a Bachelor 17
    Ballade of Book-Borrowing... 19
    Says Genial Lang... 21

TRIOLETS.

    Impromptu Triolet 25
    A Trio of Triolets... 26
    On a certain Trio of Triolets 28
    Three Triolets 29
    Two Triolets 31
    Triolet ... 32

BALLADS.

    The Wansbeck, the Wear and the Tyne ... 35
    The Ladie's Lament ... 38

CONTENTS.

	PAGE.
SONNETS.	
In Memoriam	43
A Country Ramble	44
A Night at Sea	45
An October Evening	46
Mary, Queen of Scots	47
"Love's Labour Lost"	48
MISCELLANEOUS.	
My Books: an Epistolary Fragment	51
To My Wife	55
The Unhappy Little Mouse	56
My Model Yacht	59
An Un-Æsthetic Love-Song	61
December	62
Bungo's Soliloquy	64
Hurrah for the Spring	67
A Beggar-Boy's Appeal	69
Harvest-Time	71
"The Rowfant Books"	72
A New Newcassel Sang	73
Life's Year	75
Mamma, it is Raining again	76
Rondeau	78
Mary	79
The Learned Young Miss	80
John Jones, Autograph Collector	82
L'Envoi	86

BALLADES.

Of all the songs that dwell
　Where softest speech doth flow,
Some love the sweet rondel
　And some the bright rondeau,
　With rhymes that tripping go
In mirthful measures clad:
　But would I choose them? No;
For me the blithe ballade!

　　　　　　—CLINTON SCOLLARD.

AUSTIN DOBSON—ANDREW LANG.

(Ballade à Double Refrain.)

Ah me! how many Fate makes mourn
    Unhonoured in our midst to dwell,
Tho' Epics write they, and—in scorn—
    Shun Rondeau, Ballade, Villanelle:
    Blank verse they scan—at times, as well,
In jolts and jingles harsh rhymes clang—
    But fail to reach the pinnacle
Of Austin Dobson—Andrew Lang.

Dear brothers these, whose names adorn
    Their roll who spread Poesy's spell,
Their sweetest strains heart-ward are borne
    In Rondeau, Ballade, Villanelle:
    Yet did no rival e'er excel
Their efforts in the realms o' sang;—
    The Laureate's self bears not the bell
From Austin Dobson—Andrew Lang.

Theirs not the heaviness men spurn :
    Light as the breeze in fairy dell
The flights of fancy that they turn
    To Rondeau, Ballade, Villanelle :
    From them we never flee, pell-mell,
Ne'er close their volumes with a bang ;
    O ! naught our happiness can quell
With Austin Dobson—Andrew Lang.

ENVOY.

How soothed our souls—what words can tell ?—
With Rondeau, Ballade, Villanelle :
How robb'd of many a bitter pang
By Austin Dobson—Andrew Lang.

A CHRISTMAS BALLADE.

Hurrah for Christmas time
   With its charity and cheer,
Its puddings and pantomime,
   Its flagons of home-brew'd beer,
   Its laughter loud and clear,
Its sweets for Dick and Dollie ;—
   Ah ! it comes but once a year,
Hang up mistletoe and holly.

Loudly the church-bells chime,
   Inviting all who hear
To join in praise sublime
   Of Him man holds most dear ;
   And peasant, prince and peer
Forget their melancholy,
   And—each one in his sphere—
Hang up mistletoe and holly.

To mourn would be a crime,
   Tho' the days are dark and drear,
And our ever-changing clime—
   Frequent theme of jest and jeer—
   Filleth many hearts with fear:
Now is the hearth most jolly,
   And lads—with lasses near—
Hang up mistletoe and holly.

ENVOY.

Since the weather is severe,
   Come, a little harmless folly;
Quick—ay, quick—the ladders rear,
   Hang up mistletoe and holly.

BALLADE OF UNRECOGNIZED GENIUS.

In the days of my youth I was told
   That a poet's renown would be mine,
That already my name was enroll'd
   As a protégé of the fair Nine ;
   And their praises in many a gay line
By me loud were sounded, I ween ;—
   Where now are my verses divine ?
Alas ! where wives buy butterine.

Before I was twenty years old
   Prose classics, too, did I design,
And each sketch deem'd its weight worth in gold—
   Ah me ! I my pearls cast to swine :
   As essayist hoped I to shine,
Unrivall'd by Addison e'en ;—
   Now are my effusions so fine
Alas ! where wives buy butterine.

Tho' my novels are now never sold,
    Never plagiarized over the brine,
O! the plots that I used to unfold
    Round my forehead the laurel to twine!
    But in vain still for fame do I pine—
For as yet only slated I've been,
    And my tales sent, with judicial whine,
Alas! where wives buy butterine.

ENVOY.

Sir Critic, a kind heart be thine,
    And no more spurn my volumes in spleen,
Nor—to shelve them—with others combine
    Alas! where wives buy butterine.

A TOWN-LOVER'S BALLADE.

It may be *a la mode* to rehearse the delights
   That are theirs who in rustic localities dwell,
Or to scrawl villanelles on the sounds and the sights
   That alone may be found upon moorland or fell ;
   And I own there are joys to be glean'd in a dell,
That the hay of the meadows in summer smells sweet,
   Whilst the waters are cool of a deep-seated well—
Still, I long for the stir—nay, the slush—of the street.

Mountaineers, brave and bold, sing of snow-cover'd heights,
   And the glory of climbing them oft to us tell ;—
Did the task they essay in December, their plights
   Might, perchance, soon evoke a funereal knell :
   Tho' the grunt of the pig has a musical swell,
And the cock's shrilly shriek's a melodious treat
   That to hear from their slumbers rise e'en beau and belle,
Still, I long for the stir—nay, the slush—of the street.

There's a pleasure in watching the swallow's wild flights
    As it wheels through the air that no mortal can quell,
And a pleasure in trudging the highways on nights
    When the darkness that's felt o'er our souls casts its spell:
But alas! if the Fates in their anger compel
A poor chappie to live near where sheep browse and bleat!—
Tho' in cities their manhood base men sometimes sell,
Still, I long for the stir—nay, the slush—of the street.

ENVOY.

Prince, I really believe that with rapture I'd yell
    Did my duties town-ward once again turn my feet;
Tho' 'tis years since I shouldered mankind in Pall Mall,
    Still I long for the stir—nay, the slush—of the street.

BALLADE OF A POOR BOOK-LOVER.

(*Double Refrain.*)

Tho' in its vagaries stern Fate
   A poor book-lover me decreed,
Perchance mine is a happy state—
   The books I buy I like to read :
   To me dear friends they are indeed,
But, howe'er enviously I sigh,
   Of others take I little heed —
The books I read I like to buy.

My depth of purse is not so great,
   Nor yet my bibliophilic greed,
That merely buying doth elate—
   The books I buy I like to read :
   Still, e'en when dawdling in a mead,
Beneath a cloudless summer sky,
   By bank of Tyne, or Till, or Tweed,
The books I read—I like to buy.

Their books tho' tool'd in style ornate,
  Oft worms upon the contents feed
Whilst some men of the bindings prate—
  The books I buy I like to read :
  Yet some day may my fancy breed
My ruin—it may now be nigh—
  They reap, we know, who sow the seed—
The books I read I like to buy.

ENVOY.

Tho' frequently to stall I speed,
The books I buy I like to read :
Yet wealth to me will never hie—
The books I read I like to buy.

BALLADE OF A MUFFIN-SELLER.

There's a maiden I know
　With most beauteous black eyes,
Black, in sooth, as the sloe,
　And—'twill scarce cause surprise—
　Black her hair is likewise:
In our ally she dwells,
　And—as many surmise—
　　　　　Sea-shells she sells.

From me high and low
　Purchase muffins and pies,
And when I my rounds go
　Aye my way her way lies—
　Ne'er to shun me she tries,
And with joy my breast swells
　As, beside me, she cries
　　　　　Sea-shells she sells.

E'en in famed Rotten Row,
   Ere from it Fashion flies,
No damsels e'er show
   Half the charms she supplies—
   Rivals all she outvies
As the loveliest of belles,
   Tho', wherever she hies,
          Sea-shells she sells.

ENVOY.

Fast the happy day nighs
   That all sadness dispels;
Till it's here, in Love's guise,
          Sea-shells she sells.

BALLADE ADDRESSED TO GEORGE AUGUSTUS SALA.

My rhymes are not of leafy trees,—
   Too much, alas! of them I see,
When busy lanes would better please
   And in a crowd I fain would be:
   A country life, however free
From town-temptations and excess,
   Somehow has lost its charms for me,
Great-hearted, jovial G. A. S.

It may be that I taste the lees
   Of rural innocence and glee,
And feel not health in every breeze,
   Because of Fate's most dread decree
   That robs me of the liberty
To seek anew the happiness
   Of city's stir and rivalry,
Great-hearted, jovial G. A. S.

Still, Lang and Dobson, thou and Rees,
   And thy friend Percy—altho' he
Us poor book-fanciers doth so tease
   With tales of rarities that we
   Shall never e'en behold—make flee
The solitary soul's distress,
   The void of oral sympathy,
Great-hearted, jovial G. A. S.

ENVOY.

Famed Prince of Journalists, to thee
   I turn me in my loneliness,
Fearless of failure as my fee,
   Great-hearted, jovial G. A. S.

BALLADE OF A BACHELOR.

I missed the train. Alack-a-day
  That such should be my luckless fate,
Tho' I had hurried all the way,
  Ay, hurried at a break-neck rate :
  But trains—like Time—for no man wait,
As despots do directors reign,
  The porters giggled at my strait—
            I missed the train.

I missed the train, and long shall pay
  The penalty of being late,
Tho' with wild words did I essay
  To calm my soul, for—sad to state—
  When in my face they shut the gate,
And told me to come back again,
  My manner was not quite sedate—
            I missed the train.

I missed the train, and, to allay
    My anguish and my rage abate,
Of hope found not a single ray :
    To take unto myself a mate
    My mission was—her love to hate
Changed at my absence, and in vain
    I wrote to her in terms ornate—
            I missed the train.

ENVOY.

I missed the train, but why thus prate?
    The bride of a more punctual swain
Has she become : *his* joy is great—
            I missed the train.

BALLADE OF BOOK-BORROWING.

Lender or borrower never be,
   Sings Shakespeare, but in vain he sings,
As likewise sadly singeth he
   Whose books at times seem to have wings :
   Howe'er to them his memory clings,
Howe'er their absence by him 's mourn'd,
   Naught homewards e'er the wanderers brings—
Books borrowed rarely are return'd.

O ! unaccountable to me
   How he can bear, unmoved, the stings
Of Conscience, whose dishonesty
   The most beloved of earthly things
   Would subject to vile secretings :
By *him*—ay, tho' they be but spurn'd,
   Or them aside he, ruthless, flings—
Books borrowed rarely are return'd.

Whene'er a vacuum I see
  Upon my shelves, my heart it wrings,
And I bemoan right bitterly
  My treasured volumes' vanishings :
  Still, oft within my bosom springs
The will to have the wretches burn'd
  Who keep them, altho'—e'en by kings—
Books borrowed rarely are return'd.

ENVOY.

Ye who get Books by Borrowings,
  By you be not my pleadings scorn'd,
O prove—despite my weak rhymings—
  Books borrowed *sometimes* are return'd.

SAYS GENIAL LANG.

"A lady recently sent a book of poems to Andrew Lang, who wrote in reply :—I have not had time to read the longer poems, but I admire the sonnets. Perhaps life is too short for long poems."—DAILY PAPER.

To read long poems Life's too short,
   Says genial Lang of Bookman's fame,
And, tho' a damsel fain would court
   For hers perusal, maid nor dame
   Exemption from his rule may claim ;
With Epics will the muse not flirt
   Of genial Lang of Bookman's fame :—
To read long poems Life's too short.

To read long poems Life's too short,
   Says genial Lang of Bookman's fame :
Blue China Ballades are the sort
   That charm his soul—that, without blame,
   A poet may attempt to frame ;
And sonnets sometimes bring no hurt :—
   Says genial Lang of Bookman's fame
To read long poems Life's too short.

To read long poems Life's too short,
    Says genial Lang of Bookman's fame,
In critic panoply begirt,
    A quill-arm'd knight, to put to shame
    All would-be Homers—wound and maim
Each raw-boned Pegasus :—no sport
    To genial Lang of Bookman's fame
To read long poems—Life's too short.

ENVOY.

To read long poems Life's too short,
    But then, O Prince of unknown name,
To write short poems is the *forte*
    Of genial Lang of Bookman's fame.

TRIOLETS.

Easy is the Triolet,
   If you really learn to make it!
Once a neat refrain you get,
Easy is the Triolet.
As you see! I pay my debt
   With another rhyme. Deuce take it,
Easy is the Triolet,
   If you really learn to make it.

—W. E. HENLEY.

IMPROMPTU TRIOLET :*

"Based, by the way," though, says Mr. Dobson, "on a misconception, for I did not mean that 'Northumbrians' were fiery, but only that the Percies were, as they have been since Hotspur."

Nay, nay, Mr. Dobson, it isn't quite fair
   Our temper to casually libel ;
Tho' at times with our rage we our enemies scare,
Still, my dear Mr. Dobson, it isn't quite fair
To affirm that Northumbrians a-fire are e'er—
   Not tho' they do e'en take a jibe ill :
No, no, Mr. Dobson, it isn't quite fair
   Our temper to casually libel.

* See Mr. Dobson's "Life of Goldsmith," page 104.

A TRIO OF TRIOLETS:

BY A BENEDICTINE BOOKWORM.

Books I buy—
 New and old:
Tho' poor I,
Books I buy—
For more sigh:
 Tho' wife scold,
Books I buy—
 New and old.

Books I buy—
 Old and new:
If price high,
Books I buy
On the sly—
 Oft, tho', rue:
Books I buy—
 Old and new.

Books I buy
  Of all kinds
'Neath the sky :
Books I buy—
Far and nigh
  Search for "finds":
Books I buy
  Of ALL kinds.

ON A CERTAIN TRIO OF TRIOLETS.

*Your trio is true
  As a study from life,
Whether chance (?) or you know (?)
Your trio is true,
Since here am I, too,
  With my books and--a wife!
Your trio is true
  As a study from life.*

G. W.

THREE TRIOLETS:

BY A FOND FATHER.

Herbert, Winnie, Dora, May,
  Bonnie bairns and fair are ;
Joyous, merry, laughing, gay,
Herbert, Winnie, Dora, May,
Ever drive dull care away—
  Sad or solemn ne'er are :
Herbert, Winnie, Dora, May,
  Bonnie bairns and RARE are.

Herbert, Winnie, Dora, May,
  Blue-eyed beauties all, ma'am ;
Viking-like, fond of a fray,
Herbert, Winnie, Dora, May,
With their love their mammy sway—
  "Sweets" she them doth call, ma'am :
Herbert, Winnie, Dora, May,
  Blue-eyed beauties TALL, ma'am.

Herbert, Winnie, Dora, May,
   Are their daddy's theme, sir ;
Tho' his books aside they lay,
Herbert, Winnie, Dora, May,
Every moment of the day
   Make him poet seem, sir :
Herbert, Winnie, Dora, May,
   Are their daddy's DREAM, sir.

TWO TRIOLETS:

Addressed—with a small order—to Messrs. Jarvis & Son, London.

Yestre'en arrived all right
   Your *Lytell List of Bookes*,
But with it sad delight
Yestre'en arrived;—all right
Man's lot is not, nor bright,
   When his wife angry looks:
Yestre'en arrived all right
   Your *Lytell List of Bookes*.

The wherefore and the why
   Of my wife's angry looks
You ask—dare I deny
The wherefore and the why?
She knew that I should buy
   Out of your *List of Bookes*
The wherefore and the why,
   This, of my wifie's looks.

TRIOLET.

"Ballade-mongers are piteously implored to send no more ballades."—ANDREW LANG *in "Longman's Magazine," January, 1888.*

Farewell all my hopes of renown—
   Henceforth Ballade-mongers are bann'd
At the Sign of the Ship by Lang's frown :
Farewell all my hopes of renown !
Ah me ! that thus soon should fall down
   My castles so airily plann'd :
Farewell all my hopes of renown,
   Henceforth Ballade-mongering be—bann'd.

BALLADS.

"*I love a Ballad in print, a'-life; for then we are sure they are true.*"

—A WINTER'S TALE.

THE WANSBECK, THE WEAR AND THE TYNE.

The Wansbeck, the Wear an' the Tyne,
    Three rivers that rin tae the sea,
The Wear may be dear, an' the Tyne may be dear,
    But the Wansbeck's the dearest tae me.

"May Maggie, the loveliest o' maids
    Wha dwell by the banks o' the Tyne,
Lang, lang hae I lo'ed thee, tho' silent my lo'e,
    O! wilt thou, May Maggie, be mine?"

"Nay, nay, that can be never, never;
    Never, never thou'lt claim me as thine;
But look nae sae sad, for thou ken'st verra weel
    There are monny fair maids by the Tyne."

"O! why wilt thou nae be my lo'e,
    When thy parents hae gi'en their consent?
O! why wilt thou nae be my lo'e?—
    Would'st thou see how my heart may be rent?'

"Thy lo'e I'll nay be, but thy fri'n'."—
"O! why wilt my lo'e thou nae be?—
Dost thou lo'e some ane else?"—"Nay, nay, I do nae,
But I dinna, I dinna lo'e thee."

"Wilhemina, wha liv'st by the Wear,
The dearest o' everything dear,
O! wilt thou be my ain wee wife?—
Each ither we've lo'ed this lang year."

"Ay, ay, I will be thy ain wife,
An' honour, an' lo'e, an' obey,
If my faither an' mither will gi'e their consent,
An' I dinna think they'll say nay."

"O! Minnie, thy mither says nay,
She says that we twa mauna wed;
But I lo'e, an' thou lo'est in return,
An' sae we hae naething tae dread."

"Nay, nay, if my mither says nay,
Then thou maun gi'e me back my heart;
If my mither says we mauna wed,
Alas! we are fated tae part."

"O! Jennie, o' a' the fair maids
    Wha dwell by the Wansbeck the best,
O! wilt thou accept my true lo'e,
    An' wi' thine in exchange mak' me blest?"

"Ay, I will accept thy true lo'e,
    An' mine in exchange gi'e tae thee;
'Tis months sin' I felt that my heart
    Nae langer belangèd tae me."

"But if that thy parents refuse,
    An' say that we mauna wed?"—
"O! still I'll be thine, O! still I'll be thine,
    Thine only, thine living or dead."

The Wansbeck, the Wear an' the Tyne,
    Three rivers that rin tae the sea,
The Wear may be dear, an' the Tyne may be dear,
    But the Wansbeck's the dearest tae me.

THE LADIE'S LAMENT.

O! wae is me! O! wae is me!
    For ma true love is deid,
An' rottin' awa i' th' West Countrie,
    Where th' even sky is reid.

Nae mair ma een like stars 'ill shine,
    Nae mair ma smile foak see,
Nae mair ma cheeks, like bluid-reid wine,
    Ruby an' bricht 'ill be.

Before ma true love went awa,
    Awa ti' th' West Countrie—
Where th' simmer breezes saftly blaw,
    An' th' sea sings merrilie—

He kist me ance on ither cheek,
    An' ance upon th' broo—
He kist me ance on ither cheek,
    And thrice upon the mou'.

But noo nae mair he'll kiss ma cheeks,
    Nae mair he'll kiss ma broo—
O! noo nae mair he'll kiss ma cheeks,
    An' never mair ma mou'.

Last nicht I dream'd a waefu' dream :—
    I thocht I saw ma love,
An' his face shone like th' heavenly gleam
    When on Christ alit th' dove.

Like living coals his blue een wer',
    An' braw he bair his heid,
As—moontid as only guid knights are—
    He rode on a milk-white steed.

But oot o' his briest th' reid bluid flow'd,
    Th' reid bluid flow'd amain,
An' he fetch'd a sigh as on he rode
    Over mountain and plain.

O! sad an' doon at heart he seem'd
    Until that he saw me,
Then wi' diamond blaze his twa een beam'd,
    An' he laught richt heartilie.

An' then he cried, "Alas for thee,
   An' alas for thy babe unborn,
For noo, that ma life has been ta'en frae me,
   Nae mair can I return!"

An' then he kist me on ither cheek,
   An' he kist me on ma broo—
An' then he kist me on ither cheek,
   An' thrice upon ma mou'.

An' then I wauk.—O! wae is me!
   For ma true love is deid,
An' rottin' awa i' th' West Countrie,
   Where th' even sky is reid.

SONNETS.

A sonnet is a wave of melody:
  From heaving waters of the impassioned soul
  A billow of tidal music one and whole
Flows in the "octave"; then returning free,
  Its ebbing surges in the "sestet" roll
Back to the deeps of Life's tumultuous sea.
                    —THEODORE WATTS.

IN MEMORIAM.

Lonely we feel, dear mother, since thy face
   No longer thrills us with angelic glow,
   And thy fond accents, always soft and low,
No longer cheer us onward thro' Life's race.
We miss thee much, for can there aught replace
   The care which thou for us didst hourly show?
   Yet oft are we forgetful here below,
And look for thee to find but empty space.
But why bewail our loss?—it is thy gain,
   And tho' we lose thy calm and kindly smile,
How sweet to know, how soothing in our pain,
   That we are parted only for a while :
Tho' thou art gone, and hence returnest never,
Yet we shall follow thee and stay with thee for ever.

A COUNTRY RAMBLE.

I love to ramble by a murmuring stream
    Which thro' a planta'n slowly winds along,
    To the hush'd music of its own glad song,
When the sun's rays in its bright waters gleam,
And "banks and braes" with living fragrance teem ;
    When in embracing clusters wild flowers throng,
    And wilder bees their blossoms soar among,
And earth is lovely as a mid-day dream.
My soul rejoices, and with childish glee
    I skip from flower to flower, or rest at ease
Beneath the shadow of a spreading tree,
    And listen to the hum of stream and bees :
In everything some loveliness I see—
    Sun, stream, tree, flower, all have the power to please.

A NIGHT AT SEA.

How solemn 'tis for the first time to be
   Upon the ocean all thro' a dark night,
When clouds obscure the moon, and we can see
   Around us nothing save the waters bright,
   And, in the distance, some ship's signal light;
When nothing can be heard except the glee
   Of rippling waves, and gentle breaker's sigh,
   And, at long intervals, the seagull's cry.
How awe-struck are we then, fill'd with a strange
   Yet sweet delight—sweeter than aught before;
Finding a wonderful, yet pleasing, change
   From country's stillness and from city's stir:
Then do our thoughts to things eternal range,
   Then do we feel that God is evermore.

AN OCTOBER EVENING.

Night falls apace, and, in the rubied west,
   Sol dons his crimson glories; fiery red
   The hills and heavens thitherward; o'erhead
A leaden-colour'd sky, and on its breast
Three little clouds: the breezes are at rest,
   And warblers of the woods: the only sound,
   The falling of dead leaves upon the ground,
Like sorrow's sighs by mourner scarce suppress'd,
Or the field peewit's cry, as sinks the sun
   'Neath the horizon—altogether soon
   From mortal view, but not before the moon
Peeps shyly forth, pale as a half-veil'd nun:
   So in Life's struggle, desolate and drear
Howe'er at times Man's lot, moon-like, will Hope appear.

MARY, QUEEN OF SCOTS.

Lovely thou wert, yet, tho' the poet sings
   "A thing of beauty is a joy for ever"—
   And thou in beauty hadst a rival never,
Not ev'n thy Maries that, as ivy clings
To nobler oak, clung to thee—sorrow's springs
   For thee flow'd ceaselessly; in one endeavour
   Vied man and Nature thy heart-ties to sever,
And let thee feel that Love, as Hate, has stings.
Preferr'd not Chastelâr a death of shame
   To life without thee?—Did not Bothwell make
   Himself a very devil for thy sake?—
And went not Arran mad?—Nor them we blame,
   But pity rather.—Who on thee could gaze
   And not be blinded by thy beauty's blaze?

"LOVE'S LABOUR LOST."

Of what avail are oaths when Love appears,
   And from Dan Cupid's bow the fatal dart
   With archer's aim is shot ? The stricken heart
O'erpowers the brain and fills the soul with fears ;
And, as a vessel when Destruction nears,
   Determination wavers, tho' each art
   Of Craft's evasive, soon as felt the smart,
Brought into play !—tho' smiles are changed to tears.
So Ferdinand, and Biron, and Dumain,
   And Longaville and Armado, altho'
A solemn oath ye one and all had ta'en
   " Not to see ladies—study—fast—not sleep"
   Till three short years had mingled in Time's flow,
What wonder none of you till one your oath did keep !

MISCELLANEOUS.

"*Vagrant melodies.*"

—TENNYSON.

MY BOOKS: AN EPISTOLARY FRAGMENT.

TO GLEESON WHITE.

My book-room is little, and poor are its treasures;
All pleasures are brittle, and so are my pleasures;
But though I shall never be Beckford or Locker,
While Fate does not sever the door from the knocker,
No book shall tap vainly at latch or at lattice
(If costumed urbanely, and worth our care, that is).
—EDMUND W. GOSSE.

My ambition is such
That I fain would describe, with a Dobsonesque touch,
My dearly-loved books—
Their sizes, their margins, their bindings, their looks;
But, since that cannot be,
My Muse impels me
To rehearse e'en in doggerel what chiefly I prize,
Tho' few volumes are mine a rich connoisseur buys.

First and foremost, then, I most in Ballads delight
Sung at markets and fairs—such as Goldsmith did write
When a Trinity sizar in Dublin's gay city,
Where the boys are so bold and the girls och! so witty:

The Ballads that tell how a murderer died
Confessing his fault when the gallows he spied ;
Or the troubles and cares that a lover befall
Ere the damsel he woos as his own he dares call ;
Or the woes of the wedded—their marital strife,
The wranglings and danglings of husband and wife.
And the older the Ballads the more I'm delighted,
Tho' they're "tattered and torn," still to them my love's
    plighted ;
While, if they're adorn'd with a rude cut or two,
Why—the clouds disappear that obscure the sky's blue.

From Ballads to Ballades some dullards may deem
An impossible leap, and, at first, it *does* seem—
Save to athletes alone who in training are aye—
A feat that may not be perform'd every day ;
Yet from foolhardiness I'm so rarely exempt,
(Or my courage is such !) I here make the attempt.
Well, books that do Ballades contain, tho' they savour
Of French affectation, on my shelves now find favour ;
For tho' a learn'd critic—WHAT's his name, does it
    matter ?—
With his vials of scorn and contempt did bespatter
All such "trials of skill," in the *Athenæum's* pages,
Their "blitheness," I'll warrant, his griefs oft assuages.

But Ballads and Ballades do not comprehend
All the joys that the Muses in Book-form me send;
So catholic my taste that in aught that pertains
To the fairy-like realms o'er which Fancy reigns
  I get pleasure galore—
And what can a Book-worm like me hope for more?
I own I desire—tho' æsthetic I know it's—
Editions de luxe of my favourite poets,
And poems prefer to peruse in the splendour
Of large paper copies, and think that more tender
The love-speeches are in a princeps edition—
As a beauty be-decked's a more ravishing vision,
Despite what the dreamer, so fond of his bed,
In describing Lavinia so quotably said.
But alas and alack! I have guineas so few,
And bairnies so many—bonnie bairnies, 'tis true,
Of gold worth their weight, (not a single grain less,)
But bairnies the same, that—but need I confess
That volumes expensive from my rows look not down,
Rather those you may purchase for less than a crown.

Yet at times in the air lordly castles I build,
From basement to garret with scarce volumes fill'd,
Where—in Art's highest style by the best masters bound—
Are "the books that can never be mine" by me found.

Still, one or two treasures, or what I judge such—
Tho' the reason, perchance, why I prize them so much
Applies but to myself—'mongst my other books dwell,
Rare or early editions—of whom wherefore tell?—
Well, of those to whom man in his anguish oft turns,
Of Hunt, Browning, Byron, Capern, Patmore, Burns.

Nor do poets alone constitute my " whole all "
Of the books I possess or that hold me in thrall ;
Lots of others are mine, but were I to endeavour
Half their kinds to depict I'd be taboo'd for ever :
Suffice it to say that my shelves the weight feel
Of the essays of Addison, Goldsmith, Lamb, Steele ;
And of many whom, tho' they once wrote with persistence,
Most mortals ignore as e'er having had existence.
But, in sooth, books that gentlemen's libraries may
Be without not unseldom my spirit most sway ;
Whilst of those they may not I'm not always a lover—
That they're books but in looks oftentimes I discover.

TO MY WIFE.

I.

(Inscribed in an illustrated copy of Bennett's "Sweet By-and-By.")

Tho' wedded, sweethearts we are still,
   Bound to succeed in each endeavour;
And, tho' 'a kind of heart disease,'
   Love thrills us keenlier than ever,
And proves—as on the years do fly—
Sweeter and sweeter is its By-and-by.

II.

(Inscribed in an illustrated copy of Whittier's "Maud Müller.")

Maud and the judge—unhappy twain—
WHAT MIGHT HAVE BEEN long'd for in vain:

Not hers thy lot, my lot not his,—
We are contented with WHAT IS.

THE UNHAPPY LITTLE MOUSE.

TO HERBERT, WINNIE, DORA, AND MAY.

    Once there was a little mouse
    Built a tiny little house
In the corner of a tiny little cupboard, O !
    Yet the cupboard was not bare,
    As was that, you'll be aware,
Which was owned once on a time by Mother Hubbard, O !

    There were lots of things in it
    For a monarch mousey fit
To partake of at his breakfast or his dinner, O !
    Yet ere long it came to pass
    That the little mouse, alas !
As the days and weeks went by kept getting thinner, O !

    In the cupboard there were cakes,
    Just like those mamma dear makes
On May's birthday, Winnie's, Dora's, or on brother's, O !
    There were tarts and pies as well,
    And some cheese, so nice to smell,
Little mouse preferred its odour to all others, O !

But, as I've already said,
Little mouse grew thin instead
Of increasing to the fulness of a brewer, O !
Which at first may strange appear,
Tho', when you the reason hear,
You will own that ne'er effect to cause was truer, O !

Little mouse from morn till night
Lived in flutter and in fright,
And its house dared rarely leave a single second, O !
For the owners of the cupboard
Were accustomed things to up-hoard,
And the mouse well knew that it their foe was reckoned, O !

Well it knew that if they could
Lay their hands on it they would,
And in cold blood murder it with pride and pleasure, O !
So from morning until night
Little mouse in fear and fright
Passed away the hours which years did seem to measure, O !

And from night to morn, likewise,
Mousey feared a sad surprise
From a creature whose bright eyes like diamonds glistened, O !
A fierce creature whose delight
Was to prowl about all night,
And for little mice till daybreak looked and listened, O !

So, you see, the little mouse,
In its tiny little house,
In the corner of a tiny little cupboard, O !
Had its trouble and its care,
Tho' the cupboard was not bare,
As was that, you'll be aware,
Which was owned once on a time by Mother Hubbard, O !

MY MODEL YACHT.

LITTLE HERBERT *loquitur:*

I am growing quite a sailor,
    So a vessel I have got,
Not, indeed, a great big whaler,
    But a tiny model yacht.

I have christen'd her *The Viking*,
    Tho' that she's a queen you'll wot,
Yet for carnage little liking
    Has my tiny model yacht.

I myself of her am captain—
    Mate or boatswain has she not;
And the steering I am apt in
    Of my tiny model yacht.

Scudding fast before the breezes,
    Oft it is my happy lot,
On the lake upon the Leazes
    To behold my model yacht.

Yes, I'm growing quite a sailor,
    So a vessel I have got,
And my comrades always hail her
    As a model, model yacht.

AN UN-ÆSTHETIC LOVE-SONG.

(*With apologies to* O. W.)

A barrel of beer and a glass of gin hot
   Are goodly gifts for me ;
For my own true love a half-gallon pot
   Fill'd to the brim with tea.

For thee a bloater from Yarmouth town
   (Fresh, O fresh, is a fish of the sea !) ;
For me some beef, and, to wash it down,
   A pint of porter (ah me ! ah me !).

Sherbet and zoedone for thee
   (Teetotal drinks have taking names !) ;
A cup of claret and pink for me
   (O ! men are stronger than dames !).

DECEMBER.

With Christmas chime and pantomime,
December welcomes winter-time :
With ice and snow and mistletoe,
And cheeks that red as roses glow :
With romp and rout, within, without,
And merriment's light-hearted shout :
With frozen streams, where gladness beams,
And the keen air with laughter teems,—
And maidens glide o'er the still'd tide
With chosen champions by their side,
And—full of joy without alloy—
To Love's soft whispers listen coy.

Tho' cold winds blow and rack with woe
The heart of him whose purse is low,
Yet should he not bewail his lot—
Stern Fate for all has trials got,
Which rich and poor must both endure
Ere they eternal rest secure :

Moreo'er the bells whose music swells
Each breast with hope that nothing quells,
East, west, south, north, " Peace to the earth ;
And to mankind, goodwill," ring forth :
And he who knows nor fears nor woes
Of winter-time helps him who does.

Like spectres stand o'er all the land
Gaunt, leafless trees once green and grand ;
And birds now roam across the foam
That in their branches built their home :
And the gay flowers of sunny hours
Are only seen in hothouse bowers :
Yet why should we dejected be ?—
December comes with jollity ;
With goodly cheer dispels each fear
That Nature breeds when dull or drear ;
And all mankind in love doth bind—
In love that thrills heart, soul and mind.

BUNGO'S SOLILOQUY.

I have a black retriever dog,
   A noble animal is he,
And to him I am much endeared—
      As he to me.

I got him when he was a pup,
   When scarce, indeed, a fortnight old :
Now would I not exchange him for
      His weight in gold.

I call him Bungo, which, you'll say,
   Is a strange name ; well, so it is,
At least to you, but not to me—
      For it is his.

His language, too, none understand
   Save I, yet it is plain to me,
So marvel not at this, his true
      Soliloquy :—

"Oh! what a lucky dog I am,
   Fed by a loving master's hand
Each day, upon the very best
    Of the whole land.

"A house, moreo'er, all to myself,
   The cosiest that you ever saw,
And filled, whene'er the nights are cold,
    With nice warm straw.

"My master loves me, I am sure,
   Such kindly words he speaks to me,
And, when out walking, lets me bear
    Him company :

"Sometimes, too, lets me carry what,
   I think, he calls his walking-stick ;
And he has taught me to perform
    Full many a trick.

"And, in return, him I do love,
   (For love doth ever love beget),
And always at his absence feel
    Inclined to fret.

"And so I would, but that I know
    'Twould make me lean and haggard-eyed,
And that, I wot, to him would not
        Give joy or pride.

"Yes, he does love me, I am sure,
    And often pats me on the back,
So, day and night, to please him I
        Must nothing lack.

"I'll guard his house when he's asleep,
    And thieves to steal shall not break in;
And, when he is awake, aye strive
        His praise to win."

What else dear Bungo would have said
    I am unable to report,
For, seeing me, he suddenly,
        Like gran'da's clock, stopped short.

HURRAH FOR THE SPRING.

Hurrah for the Spring, for the bountiful Spring,
To welcome whose coming the merry birds sing,
And twitter and chirp 'mid the blossoming trees ;
To greet whom the swallow re-crosses the seas
From lands where, till winter was over, it fled,
For the winds of the North fill its wee heart with dread :
  A mere speck in the sky
  Soars the glad lark on high,
And the thrush blithely pipes its sweet strains far and nigh :
Hurrah for the Spring, for the bountiful Spring,
To welcome whose coming the cuckoo doth sing.

Hurrah for the Spring, for the bountiful Spring,
That aye in its lap doth the fairest flowers bring :—
The daisy, of childhood the emblem and joy,
Bearing bliss and delight without guile or alloy ;
The primrose that shines like the brightest of gold
That the eye of a mortal did ever behold :
  The daffodil, too,
  With its soft yellow hue,
And the ladysmock white, and the violet blue :
Hurrah for the Spring, for the bountiful Spring,
That aye in its lap doth the celandine bring.

Hurrah for the Spring, for the bountiful Spring,
At whose advent the chattering rivulets fling
Airy bubbles about, so delighted are they
To resume to the ocean their musical way :
The bees, too, are humming their heartiest thanks
For the beautiful, bright honey-stores on their banks ;
   And in lake and in mere,
   With their waters so clear,
That the fishes are pleased doth most plainly appear :
Hurrah for the Spring, for the bountiful Spring,
At whose advent the bees and the brooks hum and sing.

Hurrah for the Spring, for the bountiful Spring,
That with pleasure is hailed by both beggar and king ;
For it scatters its blessings all over the land,
With prodigal, love-giving, open-palm'd hand :
By rich and by poor, and by old and by young,
Its praises are ever ecstatically sung,
   For the blood fast doth flow,
   And the palest cheeks glow,
When the end is proclaimed of the season of snow :
Hurrah for the Spring, for the bountiful Spring,
That hath blessings for beggar as well as for king.

A BEGGAR BOY'S APPEAL.

My parents died when I was young,
    When but a simple child;
And not a single soul since then
    Has e'er upon me smiled.

My only jacket is in rags,
    So long has it been worn;
My waistcoat is too big for me,
    My trousers are all torn.

No cap have I upon my head,
    No shoes upon my feet;
So I must beg the livelong day,
    In wind, and rain, and sleet.

Sometimes I get a penny-piece,
    Sometimes a crust of bread;
Yet oh! sometimes I do so wish
    That I may soon be dead.

To steal sometimes I'm tempted sore,
    But that I'll never do;
So I must beg the livelong day
    Of Christian and of Jew.

Far sooner would I work than beg,
    If work I could but get;
But no! because I'm not well dress'd
    The dog is at me set.

If none will give me work to do
    To earn my daily bread,
Then must I beg, from day to day,
    Or droop, in death, my head.

But will no person give me work?—
    For I would work with joy:
It is not alms I ask, but work—
    Work for a beggar-boy.

HARVEST-TIME.

Autumn tints appear
   On the falling leaves;
Harvest-time is here
   With its golden sheaves.

Laughter loud and long
   On the air is borne;
Willing hands and strong
   Toil amid the corn.

Fast the yellow stooks
   Into stacks are made:
O! the joyful looks
   On each face display'd!

All mankind is glad,
   Tho' the days grow drear;
How can hearts feel sad?—
   Harvest-time is here.

Yet into each soul
   May this truth sink deep:—
Till the seed is sown
   None the grain can reap.

"THE ROWFANT BOOKS."

TO FREDERICK LOCKER-LAMPSON.

The Rowfant Books,—let statesmen brawl
   For office, priests for bishops' crooks—
I'd sooner shelve against my wall
        The Rowfant Books.

A NEW NEWCASSEL SANG.

Is doon th' street th' tuthor neet
  Aw happint ti be wawkin',
Aw owortyeuk two Tyneside cheps,
  An' loodly they war tawkin':
Syed yen, "An' hev ye hard th' news?"—
  "What news?" his myet cried, turnin';
"Whei! Joe Crawhall is hard it wark
  Newcassel sangs adornin'.
        Fal de lal, etc.

"Aw's warn'd ye knaw his bits i' byeuks,
  His Chaplets an' his Garlands;
Thor fyemus for thor bonny lyeuks
  In forrin, e'en, an' far lands:
Th' funny cuts in them he puts,
  Han' cullor'd, tee, myest all, man,
Myek monny foak wi' lafter choak—
  A morderer is Crawhall, man.
        Fal de lal, etc.

"But his new byeuk when it cums oot
  Will beat them all aw'm sartin,—

Th' subject's yen wivvoot a doot
    Thit he has his hyel hart in :
Awd Cappy in his canine glee
    'Hint Ralphy toonward trottin'
Will greet yor site an' ye delite,
    But—what will thor be not in?
            Fal de lal, etc.

"Th' dog, tee, that bit Markie Dunn
    Itsel' ye'll see disportin';
An' Lizzie Mudie's ghost hoo-hoo'n ;
    An' Lukie Bessie cortin ;
Th' Keelmin gannin' ti th' church,
    Whese myestor wis relidgis,
Ti pass off for a godly man
    In hopes i' higher wages."
            Fal de lal, etc.

Just then St. Nick bigan ti strike,
    An' tell th' time iv eevin,
In tones see shrill they myed me ill,
    An' me did fairly deevin :
Aw hard nowt mair th' speaker syed,
    But ti' mesel' did sweer, sors,
Joe's byeuk ti' buy—th' price tho' high—
    Syeun is it dis ippeer, sors.
            Fal de lal, etc.

LIFE'S YEAR.

SPRING.

Children at play,
Merry and gay;
Knowing not sorrow,
Nor fearing the morrow.

SUMMER.

Slaves of Dan Cupid!
Dreadfully stupid
In worldly affairs—
Scorning Life's cares.

AUTUMN.

Husband and wife!
Settled for life;
Seeing old graces
In new forms and faces.

WINTER.

Children once more!
Life's struggles o'er:
Gloating in stealth
O'er hoarded wealth.

MAMMA, IT IS RAINING AGAIN.

"Mamma, it is raining again,
And I in the house must remain;
Oh! this is the fourth or fifth day
That I have been robb'd of my play."

"Yet weep not, my dear little boy,
All happiness has some alloy,
All pleasure is season'd with pain,
And, remember, 'tis God sends the rain."

"But, mamma dear, you know when it rains
What sorrow my bosom sustains;
You know how I love the fresh air—
Ah me! I do wish it were fair."

"Be patient, my dear little boy,
The best of good health you enjoy,
And, tho' within doors you must stay—
'Tis only until a fine day.

"Now, there is your poor cousin Jim,
So feeble and weak in each limb,
That e'en when the rain is away
He's not able to go out and play.

"Yet ne'er he his lot does bemoan,
Then why should my little boy groan,
And grumble because of the rain?"—
"Mamma, I won't do so again."

RONDEAU.

TO AARON WATSON.

Thro' lust of gold we blithely brave
The secret terrors of the grave—
   Face dangers fearlessly :—nor flee
   The cannon's mouth, the stormy sea,
The gloom of mine or pit or cave.

Yet oft as meanly we behave—
Inanely—nay, insanely—rave ;
   Shun manhood in servility—
         Thro' lust of gold.

Alas ! that we should so deprave
The nature that our Maker gave,
   And in His house, e'en, bend the knee
   Unto the idol £ s d :
Ah me ! how many a man's a knave
         Thro' lust of gold.

MARY.

She dwelt among the trodden ways
   Of London's famous city,
A maid, whom poets used to praise
   In many a doleful ditty.

Her bosom, as the lily white,
   Half visible to the eye!
Her cheeks, as when the sun at night
   Is sinking in the sky!

She lived *much* loved, yet did few know
   When Mary would be married;
But she is now a wife, and, oh!
   The hearts this fact has harried!

THE LEARNED YOUNG MISS.

There once was a learned young miss
Who found far more unalloy'd bliss
    In simple division,
    And compound addition,
Than ever she did in a kiss,
    In a kiss,
Than ever she did in a kiss.

From morning till night she would pore
O'er her books till she scarcely could stir,
    And her eyes were as red
    As the hair on her head,
And her brains were bemuddled and sore,
    'Dled and sore,
And her brains were bemuddled and sore.

She never went out for to play,
But sat at her tasks all the day,
    So, altho' she was clever,
    She was lank and lean ever,
And gradually wasted away,
    'Sted away,
And gradually wasted away.

Her friends used to tell her 'twas wrong
For people to study so long
  Without exercise,
  And their health to despise,
That they might be praised men among,
  Men among,
That they might be praised men among.

But she only replied with a grin,
And to study again would begin,
  Till, alas! one sad night
  She vanish'd from sight—
She became so exceedingly thin,
  'Dingly thin,
She became so exceedingly thin.

And from that date to this she has ne'er
By mortal been seen anywhere!—
  A warning to all
  Who contemn bat and ball
As needful in this world of care,
  World of care,
As needful in this world of care.

JOHN JONES, AUTOGRAPH COLLECTOR:

A SKETCH.

John Jones collected autographs,
And, as a man who strong ale quaffs
Finds that his thirst the more increases
The more he quaffs—at last ne'er ceases;
Or, as one of the Heber kind,
To bibliophilic tastes inclined,
Who the more volumes he possesses
His craving for them ne'er knows less is—
Buying and buying till, indeed,
He has not leisure them to read;
So Jones in tireless endeavour
His hobby whipp'd and spurr'd, nor ever
Grew weary of the chase exciting
After distinguish'd folk's handwriting.
In shops where butterine was sold
His friends did often him behold;
And in the work-rooms of men who

Trunks for a living made;—a few
Had even seen him in disguise
Searching, with keen, expectant eyes,
The refuse boxes at the doors
Of merchants and solicitors.
A letter was what most he prized,
And many were his schemes, devised
To win one to himself addressed;
And—if the truth must be confess'd,
And shamed he whose abode is Hades—
The victor's meed he ofttimes made his.
To politicians he would write,
Beseeching them for "light—more light"
Upon some burning question they
Had been elucidating—say,
Home Rule for Erin's hapless land;
Or, Compensation to the band
Of Bonifaces who had made
Enormous fortunes in a trade
Teetotallers affirm the Devil's,
And cause of more than half Earth's evils.
To poets, too, in hopes of gleaning
Some hidden or uncertain meaning,
He wrote in polish'd, well-turn'd phrases,
And—as so frequently the case is

When Flattery's tongue is set a-wagging—
And it there's seldom any gagging—
Unanswered rarely were his queries,
E'en tho' of them he ask'd a series.
To artists for their terms he sent,
Assuming it was his intent
To have his portrait ta'en, if he
Was rich enough to spare their fee,
But hinting, in a casual way,
He could their highest prices pay.
To thieves and vagabonds of note,
In hopes of a reply, he wrote:
To pugilists, who—as for fun—
Fought battles neither lost nor won:
To murderers, e'en, whose brutal crimes,
Lessening the dulness of the times,
Were welcomed by a *blasé* nation
As themes for general conversation.—
Naught came amiss to Jones's net,
He reckoned fish all he could get.
One class of autographs, howe'er,
He had no liking for; yet dare
He scarce refuse them when they came,
Tho' they that penn'd them had small fame:
These were the bills and dunning letters

That tradesmen dedicate to debtors.
Of *them* Jones had a goodly store
That, as the months went by, grew more
And more in bulk ; for tho' he'd pay
For what he fancied in the way
Of autographs, nor rue the cost,
His soul in them being so engross'd,
Yet when it came to meaner matters
With cobblers, tailors, hosiers, hatters,
He postponed payment till a day
That in the distant Future lay.—
But he is dead—Peace to his ashes !
For when he died, tho' little cash his,
To clear his debts sufficed the gold
For which his autographs were sold.

L'ENVOI.

A BALLADE OF ENFORCED IMPECCABILITY.

When the Corinthians heard that Philip was going to attack them . . . they fell to work, . . . every one lending a hand; but DIOGENES *observing this, and having nothing to do* (FOR NOBODY EMPLOYED HIM), *fell a-rolling his tub up and down the Cranium.*—LUCIAN.

To you, DEAR SIR, *at your request,*
Some half-a-score of lines addressed
For ENVOY, *I had planned to write,*
When lo! my LUCIAN *that same night*
Warned me of such a dire offence
To 'newest journalism's' sense.
Yet since DIOGENES *was seen*
In equal straits, and though it's mean
To take advantage of a Greek,
Behind his tub, I refuge seek—
Willing to praise, but nobody
Wants of my praise—so poor I be.

L'ENVOI.

Though I should laud you to the skies
Not one more churl your volume buys;
While if I damned, as critics do,
'Twould hurt not you—'twould NOT *hurt you.*

I.

To roll their logs would please me well,
   But then alack! they won't roll mine:
' Spectator,' ' Saturday,' ' Pall Mall,'
   Print of my work no single line;
No one invites me out to dine,
Or even 'slates' me,—there's the rub;
   No tapers burn before my shrine:—
They roll their logs—I'll roll my tub!

II.

If but their bribes I could repel
   With virtue brave, if superfine,
Or if my books would only sell,
   Then might I fit with their design:
But no one makes the faintest sign,
Me, and my books, alike they snub—
   No flatteries can I decline—
They roll their logs—I'll roll my tub!!

III.

Yet in no solitary cell,
  Meek, hermit-like, will I repine;
Since by myself I needs must dwell,
  The lean shall slang the fatter kine,
  And sneer at what they all combine
To praise in esoteric club.
  Across their walnuts and their wine
They roll their logs.—I'll roll my tub!!!

ENVOY.

Virtue, impeccable, divine,
  Behold in me! The rest I dub
Log-rolling scribblers—so I shine—
  They roll their logs—I'll roll my tub.

—G. W.

THE END.

DERBY AND NOTTINGHAM: FRANK MURRAY.

By the same author: uniform with the present volume.

TO BE PUBLISHED NEXT YEAR.

JOLTS AND JINGLES
A BOOK OF POEMS FOR YOUNG PEOPLE

BY

THOMAS HUTCHINSON

Author of "Ballades of a Country Bookworm."

The Edition will be entirely on Hand-made Paper, and will be limited to

120 Copies in Foolscap 8vo., and
50 Copies, Large Paper, in Demy 8vo.,

NUMBERED AND SIGNED.

About 80 pp., elegantly printed, and bound in limp parchment.

Subscribers' Names should be sent at once to the Publishers.

Price (in advance), 3/- ; Large Paper, 6/-.

On the day of publication the price will be raised to 4/6 and 9/- respectively.

LONDON:
STANESBY & CO., 179, SLOANE STREET, S.W.
(FORMERLY MURRAY & STANESBY).

DERBY AND NOTTINGHAM:
FRANK MURRAY.

www.ingramcontent.com/pod-product-compliance
Lightning Source LLC
Chambersburg PA
CBHW031619170426
43195CB00037B/1274